DISCOVER

SNAKES

Titles in the *Discover Animals* series:

Discover Big Cats
ISBN-13: 978-0-7660-3473-0
ISBN-10:   0-7660-3473-9

Discover Bugs
ISBN-13: 978-0-7660-3472-3
ISBN-10:   0-7660-3472-0

Discover Sharks
ISBN-13: 978-0-7660-3474-7
ISBN-10:   0-7660-3474-7

Discover Snakes
ISBN-13: 978-0-7660-3471-6
ISBN-10:   0-7660-3471-2

DISCOVER ANIMALS

DISCOVER

SNAKES

Sujatha Menon

Enslow Publishers, Inc.
40 Industrial Road
Box 398
Berkeley Heights, NJ 07922
USA
http://www.enslow.com

Library of Congress Cataloging-in-Publication Data

Menon, Sujatha.
Discover snakes / Sujatha Menon.
p. cm. — (Discover animals)
Previously published: [S.l.] : Really Useful Map Company, c2005.
Includes bibliographical references and index.
Summary: "Learn about the different kinds of snakes that are located
all over the world, from rattlers to pythons to harmless
snakes"—Provided by publisher.
ISBN 978-0-7660-3471-6
1. Snakes—Juvenile literature. I. Title.
QL666.06M47 2008
597.96—dc22
                                          2008013867

Printed in China

10 9 8 7 6 5 4 3 2 1

To Our Readers: We have done our best to make sure all Internet Addresses in this book were active and appropriate when we went to press. However, the author and the publisher have no control over and assume no liability for the material available on those Internet sites or on other Web sites they may link to. Any comments or suggestions can be sent by e-mail to comments@enslow.com or to the address on the back cover.

Enslow Publishers, Inc., is committed to printing our books on recycled paper.
The paper in every book contains 10% to 30% post-consumer waste (PCW).
The cover board on the outside of each book contains 100% PCW.
Our goal is to do our part to help young people and the environment too!

Photo and Illustration Credits: Q2AMedia

Cover Photos and Illustrations: Q2AMedia

Contents

Serpent Tale

Snakes are feared for their deadly venom and humans often kill them for this very reason. But what most of us do not know is that these reptiles are shy and prefer to escape when threatened. There are over 2,500 species of snakes. They vary in size, shape, color and pattern.

Bones and organs

Snakes are vertebrates - they have a backbone made of small bones called vertebrae. They have a heart, a stomach, a liver, lungs, kidneys and intestines.

Legless and cold-blooded

It is the lack of legs that separates snakes from other animals. Scientists believe that snakes descended from lizards that shed their legs millions of years ago. To make up for their lack of legs, snakes have developed an efficient slithering movement. Snakes are also cold-blooded – they do not generate heat and have to bask in the sun to keep themselves warm.

■ Snakes have 100-500 vertebrae in their body. This large vertebral column provides the snake with great flexibility for movement. A pair of tiny ribs are attached to each vertebra. However, the vertebrae in the tail lack ribs.

INTERESTING FACT!

Snake venoms have enzymes that may be used to produce medicines in the future. In fact, snake bites are effectively treated with the help of snake venom!

■ Boas and pythons eat a wide range of warm-blooded animals, from rodents to birds and deer. The larger the prey the longer it takes to swallow and digest it.

Gobble up the rats

Snakes have an important task in the cycle of nature. They control the population of rats, mice, lizards and pests. These creatures destroy crops and stored food. Their uncontrolled growth also leads to plagues, infections and other health hazards.

Going in for the kill

Snakes kill when they're hungry or when attacked. Most bite their prey, while some, like vipers, rattlesnakes and cobras, also inject venom that can be fatal. Larger ones like boas and pythons wrap their body around their prey and suffocate it.

■ The jaws of a snake are not rigidly attached to its skull. Instead, they are linked to the skull by muscles and ligaments. This helps the snake to open its jaws as wide as it wants while eating.

Evolution of Snakes

Where did snakes come from? Did they crawl out of the sea? Were they reptiles burrowing holes in the ground? Like all living creatures, snakes have undergone evolution. Evolution is the process by which the traits of a species change over a long period of time, as animals with the traits best suited to their environment survive and reproduce. Most scientists believe snakes evolved from lizards nearly 270 million years ago, but some think they were originally marine creatures.

Snakes and lizards

The study of fossils suggests that snakes evolved from lizards. They share a similar skull structure and a movable jaw. It is believed that over millions of years, a family of lizards that buried holes in the ground lost its limbs and external ears. They then came to the surface and developed the slithering movement.

■ Legless lizards can easily be mistaken for snakes. But unlike snakes, these creatures have movable eyelids and external ears.

Rising from the sea

Some biologists believe that the unique features of snakes developed because they lived in water. The lack of ears, scale-covered eyes and long limbless bodies allowed the first snakes to swim efficiently. It was much later that they slithered on to dry land. Scientists also believe that snakes and monitor lizards, such as the Komodo dragon, are related. It is said that the Pachyrhachis, which gave rise to modern snakes, evolved from mosasaurs, ancestors of monitor lizards.

FACT FILE

Ancestor
Pachyrhachis
Existed
over 100 million years ago
Found in
Asia, in Israel
Grew up to
3 feet (1 m)
Habitat
lived in water

■ Some snakes like the python have traces of hind limbs. These limbs, called spurs, support the theory that snakes evolved from lizards.

Striking with venom

Millions of years ago, most early snakes disappeared due to changes in climate. But some survived by developing new traits like enlarged teeth and a venom sac. These snakes started to bite and inject poison into their prey to make killing easier.

The modern snake

The fight for survival continued. When the modern vipers appeared, they had long tongues to sense prey from a distance, and heat-sensitive pits to hunt at night. Finally, a few million years ago, some snakes developed a bone structure at the tail-end that could be rattled to warn predators. Rattlesnakes are the most specialized of all snakes.

Snakes, Snakes Everywhere

Based on their skeletal structure, snakes have been divided into over 15 families. Of these, the colubrids, elapids, vipers, pit vipers, boas and pythons are well known.

■ This brightly colored blood-red corn snake belongs to the colubrid family and is quite harmless.

Colubrids

Snakes of the *Colubridae* family are popularly called colubrids. There are around 1,800 species in this category, making it the largest snake family. Colubrids include most of the harmless snakes, such as the rat snake, the common water snake and the grass snake.

Elapids

The *Elapidae* family comprises over 250 species of snakes, all of which are poisonous. Elapids are commonly referred to as the cobra family. This family includes all cobras, kraits, mambas and coral snakes.

■ Although they resemble vipers, death adders are actually elapids. They are extremely poisonous and are found in almost all parts of Australia.

Vipers and pit vipers

Vipers are divided into two main groups – true vipers and pit vipers. The *Viperidae* family is made up of 50 species of true vipers. A Russell's viper is a kind of true viper. Pit vipers belong to the *Crotalinae* family. There are around 100 species in this family. They can be distinguished from vipers by the heat-detecting pits between their eyes and nostrils. Rattlesnakes and bushmasters are pit vipers.

■ The *Pythonidae* family consists of 30 species of pythons. The reticulated python is the longest snake in the world.

Boas and pythons

Anacondas and boas belong to the *Boidae* family. Of the 70 species, most have large, muscular bodies and kill their prey by coiling around it. The anaconda, a water boa, is considered to be the heaviest snake. Pythons belong to a sub-family of *Boidae*. They, too, kill their prey by suffocating it.

INTERESTING FACT!

Snakes of the *Boidae* family are believed to be the oldest in the world. They existed even during the age of dinosaurs. The snakes of this family are the only ones that possess two lungs, instead of just one elongated lung!

Know Your Fangs

One of the easiest ways of identifying the different kinds of snakes is by their teeth and fangs. The structure and arrangement of these differ from family to family. Most poisonous snakes have two hollow fangs attached to the upper jaw. Depending on their teeth and fangs, snakes are broadly classified into four groups.

■ Although most rear-fanged snakes are not dangerous to humans, the bite of African boomslangs can be fatal.

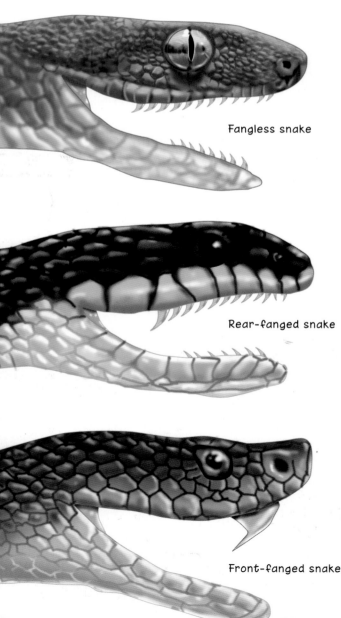

Fangless snake

Rear-fanged snake

Front-fanged snake

Fangless snakes

These snakes are called *Aglyphs*, and they do not have fangs to inject poison. However, they have several large teeth curved inward. This helps in gripping prey while killing it. Fangless snakes include blind snakes, pythons, boas, and some colubrids.

Rear-fanged snakes

Snakes in this category are known as *Opistoglyphs*, and they have two to four long fangs. As the name suggests, these fangs are placed toward the back of the snake's mouth. A number of colubrids make up this group.

Front-fanged snakes

Almost all elapids are front-fanged, or *Proteroglyphs*. Their fangs are fixed. Since they cannot be folded the fangs have to be short – making sure that the snake does not bite itself when it closes its mouth. The cobra is the most famous of front-fanged snakes.

■ The long fangs of pit vipers help them to inject the poison deep into the body of the prey.

Fang sheath
Venom gland
Venom duct
Hollow rectractable fangs
Eye
Nostril
Heat sensing pit

Pipe-grooved snakes

All vipers and pit vipers fall under this category. They are called *Solenoglyphs*. These snakes have long fangs attached to the front of the upper jaw. These fangs can be moved at will, and are kept folded when not in use.

Extendable glottis allows breathing while ingesting prey.

Forked tongue

Small curved teeth

INTERESTING FACT!

The Gaboon viper of Africa has the longest fangs. They can grow up to 2 inches (5 cm) in length. Interestingly, the Gaboon viper's venom is not as toxic as some of the other species'.

A Scaly Tale

Snakes have a long and cylindrical body and their bone structure and organs are adjusted to this shape. The body of the snake is covered with dry scales. Bigger scales on the belly help in gripping the ground.

The whole length

The slender body of snakes is ideal for slithering and creeping into small holes. Since snakes are long and narrow, paired organs like lungs and kidneys are placed one in front of the other. Most snakes have a single, narrow lung that does the work of two. In some sea snakes, this lung stretches along the entire body to keep the snake afloat.

■ It is easy to identify snakes by studying the unique patterns on their scales. For instance, the Indian cobra has a spectacle-shaped pattern on its hood, which distinguishes it from other snakes in the family.

INTERESTING FACT!

Snakes cannot close their eyes! This is because they do not have movable eyelids. The snake's eyes are protected by a special transparent scale called the brille or spectacle!

■ This African egg-eating snake can swallow eggs, even three times the size of its head! This is made possible by its special jaws and extra folds of skin, which provide the snake with its flexibility.

Shaped to adapt

Snakes have different body shapes depending on their habitat. Snakes like vipers and cobras have circular bodies with strong muscles. This helps them to get a better grip on sand and rocks. Water snakes and sea snakes have a flattened body with a paddle-like tail that helps them to push through water.

Brand new skin

The outer layer of skin becomes old over time and has to be replaced regularly. This is done by shedding it after a new, healthy layer has developed underneath. This is called molting. Some snakes molt every 20 days, while others do it only once a year.

■ To remove its old skin, the snake breaks it by rubbing itself against a rock or any other rough surface. It then crawls out of the dead skin, turning it inside out.

Scales that tell tales

One can tell where a particular snake lives by looking at its scales. Snake scales can be rough or smooth depending upon the snake's environment. Snakes that live in wetlands, marshes and rivers have keeled (ridged) scales that help the snakes to balance themselves in the wet surroundings. Some water and sea snakes have rough sandpaper-like scales that help them to grip their prey better. Burrowing snakes have smooth scales, which enable them to move through soil easily.

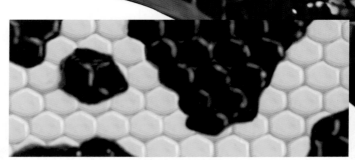

Smooth Skin

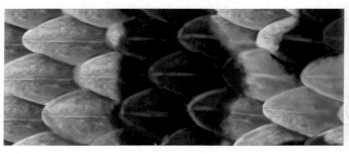

Rough Skin

Sharp Senses

Snakes rely on a number of senses like smell, heat, sight, sound and touch. Some have more refined senses than others. Through millions of years of evolution, snakes have developed senses that are unique in the animal world. Most of these features came about since they live at ground level and do not have legs.

■ There is a small opening on the upper lip that enables the snake to flick its tongue in and out without having to open its mouth.

More than a nose

Snakes have a nose, but they possess another advanced organ for detecting scents. Their forked tongue picks up chemical traces and transfers them into pits on the roof of the mouth. These pits, called Jacobson's organ, analyze the chemicals and help the snake to identify its prey.

Sound and touch

Snakes do not have external ears, but they can hear. Ground vibrations are transmitted through the body to a bone that connects the lower jaw and the skull. An inner ear then picks up the vibrations. Snakes are also very responsive to touch.

Brain

Nerve

Jacobson's organ

Forked tongue

Eye

Nostril

California night snake

Turn on the heat

Certain snakes, like the California night snake, are able to sense the heat of other creatures. This is most developed in vipers, pythons and boas. Heat-detecting sensors pick up the difference in temperatures between the prey and the surroundings. That is how snakes can strike even in the dark.

INTERESTING FACT!

Certain animals, such as Siberian chipmunks, smear themselves with snake urine or roll over dead snakes so that they smell like snakes. Studies have revealed that snakes are less likely to attack prey which have a smell like their own!

Whip snake
[day hunter]

Prey spotting

Most snakes have good eyesight, but they get a limited view because they are ground creatures. They are good at detecting movement but weak at identifying colors. The eyes of snakes are also adapted to their surroundings. Tree snakes that catch birds have large pupils, similar to those that hunt at night. Some burrowing snakes like blind snakes have eyes that only distinguish between light and darkness.

Horned viper
[night hunter]

■ Snakes that are active at night usually have small eyes, while those that hunt during the day have large eyes. Some snakes like the vine snake even have 3D vision, since their eyes are located at the front of their head.

On the Move

Snakes have developed an efficient way of moving about that more than makes up for their lack of legs. The slithering movement may suggest that they do not have bones. In fact, they actually use their bones, muscles and scales to move. The muscles help the ribs pull the scales forward and backward, which in turn helps in locomotion. Snakes move in four different ways.

Rectilinear movement

Serpentine movement

Concertina movement

■ The brown tree snake uses the concertina movement to climb trees. It first coils its tail around a branch, using the neck to cling on to a higher branch. The snake then pulls up the rest of its body.

Serpentine movement

Most snakes use serpentine motion, also called lateral or side-to-side undulation. They produce muscular waves by tightening and relaxing a set of muscles. The tail pushes against the surface. The two actions together thrust the snake forward in an 'S' pattern. Some snakes can move at speeds of 6.2 mph (10 km/h) in this fashion.

Concertina

In this movement the snake anchors the front of its body to the surface and pulls up the rest of its body. It then uses this part to push the front part forward, like a caterpillar. Most snakes use this movement to climb trees and to move through narrow spaces.

Desert snakes, like the sidewinder rattlesnake, use the sidewinding motion. Only small parts of the snake's body touch the hot ground, giving the appearance that the snake is jumping.

FACT FILE

The flying snake does not 'fly'. It 'glides' from one branch to another.
It can glide up to a distance of 328 feet (100 m)!
The flying snake uses lateral undulation, or the serpentine movement, to glide.
Snakes cannot move backwards. They have to turn their heads around and then pull their body behind it.
But snakes can strike at something behind them by merely moving their heads.

Sidewinding

This is a spectacular movement that snakes use to move on sandy surfaces. They anchor their heads on the ground and push the body sideways after forming an arc. A part of the body travels through the air before touching the sand.

Sidewinder movement

Rectilinear

Large snakes such as boas and pythons move in this manner. They extend the scales under their belly to push against the ground and move in a fairly straight line.

■ Sea snakes and other water snakes use the lateral movement to swim in water. They push their sides against the water and use their paddle-like tails for additional thrust.

INTERESTING FACT!

The poisonous yellow-bellied sea snake can swim at more than 1.86 mph (3 km/h). It is the fastest among sea snakes, and lives along the Pacific Coast of North America.

Family Tree

Snakes are not very social. They prefer to live and hunt alone. It would be unusual to see a father snake, a mother snake, and their young together.

■ Baby rattlesnakes are as dangerous as the adults. They have short fangs with venom right from the time they are born.

INTERESTING FACT!

Female rattlesnakes are sometimes killed while the babies are still inside her. This has given rise to the myth that mother rattlesnakes swallow their babies to protect them from predators.

Happy birthday

Snakes have two different ways of giving birth. Most of them lay eggs, from which the babies later hatch. Such snakes are called *oviparous*. Some do not lay eggs. Instead, the babies hatch inside the mother, who then gives birth to her young. These snakes are *ovoviviparous*.

Eggs-actly!

Snakes' eggs are soft, tough and leathery. The shell is not hard like birds' eggs. The babies take some time to wriggle out of them. The mother lays the eggs in damp and warm spots, and tries to hide them from egg-eating predators.

■ Most birds of prey eat snakes. Eagles and owls are known to feed on both adult snakes and their young.

Mama's love

Mother snakes are not very caring. They do not stay long with their newborns. But there are exceptions. The Indian python, for example, is very protective of its eggs. The snake coils its body around the eggs and shivers to keep them warm. King cobras make elaborate nests for their eggs.

Young and brave

Newborn snakes are fiercely independent, and can take care of themselves. In some cases, they can be more venomous than their parents. They also shed their skin more frequently. Since they are small, young snakes are always in danger of being hunted by birds and other snakes. Kingsnakes and cobras feed on smaller snakes.

■ A new-born emerald tree boa is usually red or orange in color. In the course of one year, the snake slowly turns golden yellow before turning completely green. This phenomenon is known as Juvenile polymorphism. The green color of the adult snake keeps getting darker as it grows older.

Attack and Defense

Most snakes are not aggressive by nature. They strike only for food and to defend themselves. Since they do not have legs, snakes have developed unique tactics to hunt and protect themselves.

Strike mode

The most common form of attack is to bite the prey. Snakes like the cobra rise high above the ground while striking. But most snakes, such as vipers and pit vipers, creep up slowly and quietly, and strike swiftly when the prey is within reach. If there is a chance of the prey being dangerous, a snake will bite and release it, waiting for the venom to work.

■ Most poisonous snakes inject their venom into the prey and wait for it to die. But some of them swallow their prey alive. Most tree snakes, like this parrot snake, hold on to the branches with their tail and swallow their prey upside down!

■ The venom of a cobra, a neurotoxin, affects the nervous system. The venom paralyzes the nerves that control the heart and the respiratory system. Cobras are immune to venom produced by their own kind.

Deadly coils

Snakes like boas and pythons are not poisonous. They have other ways of killing their prey. These snakes wrap their body around their prey in coils. The coils are slowly tightened until the victim suffocates and dies. Anacondas are sometimes known to drag their prey underwater and drown it.

Retreat policy

Snakes are naturally equipped for defense. Camouflages in earth tones make it tough for predators to spot them. For instance, some tree snakes are as green as leaves, and will hide and remain still when they are in danger. Certain snakes, such as the false coral snake, mimic the color patterns of poisonous snakes to fool attackers. Some cobras have false eye spots on the back of their head to scare predators away. However, most snakes prefer to escape to safety if they are alerted in time.

■ Both these snakes are found in Central America. They have the same color and bands that make them look like identical twins! But upon closer examination one will notice that the false coral snake's tail has red in it, unlike the yellow and black tail of the coral snake.

INTERESTING FACT!

The Chinese martial art *t'ai chi* is said to be inspired by the speed and controlled movement of snakes. *T'ai chi* is all about reflexes, flexibility, balance and concentration. It is a popular form of relaxation and self-defense.

The rattle of the rattlesnake.

Innovations

Snakes have special defense techniques. The most famous, of course, is the rattlesnake, which rattles its scaly tail to make a loud noise. The cobra raises its hood and hisses in warning. Some harmless snakes open their mouth wide to scare their attackers. The hog-nosed snake can even pretend to be dead!

The Cobra

The cobra is famous for its deadly bite and its raised, expandable hood. When disturbed, it flares this hood and creates a scary yet fascinating image. Several varieties of cobras are found throughout Asia and Africa.

King cobra

This is the world's longest venomous snake. It is, on average, 12 feet (3.6 m) long, but is known to grow up to 18 feet (5.5 m). It is olive or brown in color and often has yellow or white bands. It makes a low hissing sound that sounds more like a dog's growl. The king cobra's hood lacks a pattern, distinguishing it from other cobras. The king cobra has to rise while attacking because it can only strike downward. In fact, it can rise up to 6 feet (1.8 m) – that is as tall as a full-grown man!

The king's venom

The venom of the king cobra is not as strong as other cobras. But it is feared because it injects more poison when it bites. It mostly feeds on other snakes, and does not attack humans unless disturbed. Enough of its poison could kill an elephant.

■ The Egyptian banded cobra, or asp, is found along the northern coast of Africa. Ancient Egyptians believed that this snake could spit fire. Pharaohs used the snake as a protective symbol on their crowns. It is believed that Cleopatra killed herself by making an asp bite her tongue.

■ The king cobra is the only snake that makes nests for its eggs. The female king cobra uses leaves, twigs and soil to make nests in bamboo groves.

Spitting cobra

This snake can spray venom from a distance of about 8 feet (2.5 m) into the eyes of its victims, causing temporary blindness. The black-necked spitting cobra and the Mozambique spitting cobra are well known.

HABITAT

FACT FILE

Family
Elapidae
Lifespan
20 years
Habitat
Southern Asia and Africa
Longest poisonous snake
king cobra 12-18 feet
(3.6-5.5 m)
Smallest cobra
ringhals 4 feet (1.2 m)

■ Spitting cobras usually spray out venom droplets only as a form of defense. When capturing prey, these cobras have to bite to inject venom.

Spectacled and monocled cobra

The spectacled cobra is also known as the Indian cobra. It has a double eyeglass-shaped pattern on the back of its head. Its hood is much larger than the king cobra's. The monocled cobra has a similar pattern on its hood, but with a single (mono) ring.

INTERESTING FACT!

Oriental snake-charmers entertain people by making the snake sway to the music of their flute. But the cobra cannot hear the tune. It actually reacts to the movement of the flute.

■ Although the spectacled, or Indian, cobra causes a huge number of human deaths, its venom is used in painkillers and also in the development of antivenin.

Mambas and Kraits

Both mambas and kraits belong to the cobra family. Mambas are long, swift and poisonous snakes found in Africa. They have big eyes. Most of them prefer to stay on trees. Kraits are found only in Asia. They are slender and have a narrow head.

■ During the spring season, male black mambas can be seen fighting. They raise and intertwine their bodies during combat, which is often mistaken for mating.

Black mamba

This is the most well-known of all mambas and is feared by humans because of its speed and venom. Despite its name, the black mamba is not actually black in color. It has a brownish-gray body with a light belly. It gets its name from the purple-black lining in its mouth, which is displayed when the snake feels threatened. The black mamba feeds on small mammals and birds, and spends more time on the ground. Black mambas are normally found in pairs or groups.

Green mamba

The bright green color of this mamba helps it to hide in trees. It feeds on small birds and lizards. Unlike the black mamba, the green mamba travels alone. The Eastern green mamba is the smallest in the mamba family.

FACT FILE

Length of the black mamba
9.8-13 feet (3-4 m)
Length of the green mamba
4- 7 feet (1.2-2 m)
Litter size of the green mamba
10 to 15 babies
Length of the banded krait
8 feet (2.4 m)
Litter size of the banded krait
10 to 12 babies

■ Kraits live very close to human habitats. They also show a tendency to hide in shoes, tents and sleeping bags. Most of the attacks involving kraits are accidental due to this particular behavior.

Common krait

This snake is generally slate-colored with thin white bands. It can grow up to 6 feet (1.8 m). The common krait frequents open grasslands and semi-arid regions. They are also seen in cultivated fields and in wet areas, such as near wells and tanks.

Banded krait

The banded krait has alternate black and yellow bands. It is commonly found in India. Like most kraits, it often eats other snakes, including its own kind.

INTERESTING FACT!

Krait venom is 15 times stronger than the cobra's. Yet kraits are not considered as dangerous since they are not at all aggressive. They prefer to laze around in the day and will not bite without good reason.

Coral Snakes and Sea Snakes

Coral snakes are found in Central and South America. They are small but highly venomous and very colorful. Sea snakes are most common in the warm waters of the Indian and Pacific oceans. They are not very long, but can be ten times more venomous than rattlesnakes. Coral snakes and sea snakes also belong to the *Elapidae* family.

■ Not all coral snakes have colorful bands. In albino coral snakes the bands might be completely absent, or the black bands might be gray or missing. The yellow and red bands could either be normal or very faint.

Coiled tales

Coral snakes, with their red, orange, yellow and black bands, are very attractive. But these snakes are seldom seen because they hunt at night. Coral snakes have small and fixed fangs and they bite only when attacked. They have a habit of curling up in tight coils when threatened.

INTERESTING FACT!

Sea snakes can spend long periods underwater because they have a lung that extends almost throughout the length of their body. They can also breathe through their skin.

Sea krait

This is the largest of all sea snakes and is found in most oceans, except the Atlantic. The sea krait is also well-adapted to living on land. It goes ashore to digest its food and shed its skin. The sea krait also returns to land to mate and lay eggs.

■ The yellow-bellied sea snake is the only true sea snake. It never leaves the water to come to the shore. At night, this snake dives to the bottom of the sea and can stay there for almost three hours before coming up to the surface to breathe.

■ Coral snakes lay a clutch of eggs in the summer. The babies hatch about 60 days later.

■ Diamondback water snakes are known to swim through water with their mouths open and swallow as many fish and other smaller creatures as possible.

Yellow-bellied sea snake

As its name suggests, this snake has a bright yellow belly. Although it is one of the most poisonous snakes, it attacks only when disturbed. The yellow-bellied sea snake is the fastest of all sea snakes.

Vipers

Vipers are highly evolved venomous snakes. They belong to the *Viperidae* family, and are found in most tropical regions of the world except Australia. They are also known as true, or Old World, vipers. Unlike pit vipers, or New World vipers, they do not have heat-detecting pits.

Usambara bush viper

■ Eyelash pit vipers and the Usambara mountain bush viper look very similar. Both live on trees and have pointed scales above their eyes that look like eyelashes. Even their colors are similar. However, the Usambara bush viper lacks heat sensors, making it a true viper.

Eyelash pit viper

Fearful fangs

Vipers have developed a sophisticated system of survival. They have big, hollow fangs that can be folded into the roof of the mouth when not in use. The venom is delivered through these fangs when the snake bites. The fangs are so sharp and the poison so powerful that often one bite is enough to kill the prey.

Russell's viper

This dangerous snake is abundant in Southeast Asia. Its bite is extremely venomous and is responsible for the greatest number of human deaths. The Russell's viper is not very long but it is fast and accurate.

FACT FILE

Length of the Russell's viper
3.3-4.9 feet (1m to 1.5 m)
Habitat of the Gaboon viper
dense rainforests of Africa
Weight of the Gaboon viper
18 pounds (8 kg)
Distribution of adders
throughout Europe

Gaboon viper

Also called the Gabon viper, its fangs are the longest among all snakes – as big as 2 inches (5 cm)! It is the biggest among Old World vipers, and can grow to almost 6.6 feet (2 m). It is a ground-dwelling snake, and is excellent at camouflaging itself among leaves.

INTERESTING FACT!

The viper's venom is harmless as long as it does not enter the bloodstream.

Adder

The best known of this variety is the common adder, or the common European viper. Despite its venom, the adder is not aggressive. It is the only poisonous snake in England, and is less than 3 feet in length.

Most vipers adopt a wait-and-watch approach to capture prey. Some, like this desert horned viper, resort to camouflage tactics. The snake buries itself in the sand, lying still for the prey to come close. Only its head can be seen above the sand.

Pit Vipers

Pit vipers are a New World family of poisonous snakes. Like Old World vipers, they too have long fangs. But it is their pits, or heat-detecting organs, that make the pit vipers really unique. Most pit vipers are extremely poisonous and will strike when disturbed.

Copperhead

The copperhead is one of the least dangerous venomous snakes in the U.S. It is not very aggressive and has weak venom. Copperheads are very attractive. They are found in several colors, such as brown, pink, orange or yellow. A bright yellow or orange line is found near the mouth.

■ A female bushmaster lays her eggs in burrows built by other animals. Sometimes, the bushmaster even shares the burrow with the particular animal. After laying the eggs, the snake guards them until they hatch. During this period of over 70 days, she does not leave the burrow even to hunt!

Bushmaster

This is the longest poisonous snake in South America. It is believed to be the world's largest pit viper, and can grow to more than 10 feet (3 m). Its scales are rough, and it is usually brown or pink in color. The bushmaster prefers undisturbed tropical forests. The thick foliage provides these snakes with good protection from predators.

Fer-de-lance

This is yet another infamous pit viper from Central and South America. It is known by several names, such as yellow-jaw, yellow tail and barba amarilla. Its venom is believed to have caused more human deaths than any other American snake. It mainly lives on the ground, but also occasionally climbs trees and swims. Fer-de-lances have dark arrowhead markings on their body and can blend into their surroundings very well.

■ The heat-detecting pits of pit vipers are located between the eyes and nostrils.

Pit

Bad-tempered pit vipers

Some pit vipers are very aggressive. The mangrove or shore pit viper, the eyelash pit viper, and the Habu pit viper may strike without warning. They have very strong venom, which can be fatal.

INTERESTING FACT!

A snake's venom helps it to digest its food faster. The more venom, the faster the digestion. It has been found that without its venom a fer-de-lance would take twice the time to digest its meal.

■ The cottonmouth, commonly known as water moccasin, gets its name from the white color inside its mouth. If threatened this snake often opens its mouth, displaying this feature.

The Rattlers

The rattlesnake is a kind of pit viper that is found in the U.S., Canada and Mexico. It has heat-detecting pits and folding fangs. But what is most interesting about the snake is the rattle at the end of its tail. The rattlesnake uses this to warn its attackers.

Famous rattlers

The Eastern diamondback rattlesnake is the largest of its kind. It is the most venomous snake in the U.S. The smallest rattlers are the ridge-nosed and the pygmy rattlesnakes. The Santa Catalina rattlesnake does not have a rattle at all! The sidewinder has an interesting movement – it hurls its body in loops across the hot sand.

Beware!

The rattle is actually made up of a series of hard ring-like scales, connected to each other. When the snake shakes it tail, the scales move across each other to produce a loud rattling sound that can be heard from a distance.

HABITAT

FACT FILE

Rattlesnakes usually live and hunt alone.
But in winters they hibernate in huge numbers.
Varieties there are 16 different varieties of rattlesnakes.
Litter size 9 to 10 babies
Length of the Eastern diamondback rattlesnake 3.5-8 feet (1-2.4 m)

■ Strangely, the rattlesnake does not use its rattle when it comes across a kingsnake. Instead, it raises the front part of its body to appear bigger. But the kingsnake (in the picture on the left) is not frightened by this behavior and swallows the rattler!

Rattle tale

A rattlesnake is not born with a rattle. A newborn rattler only has a "button" at the tip of its tail. Every time it sheds its skin, a ring is added to form the rattle. Sometimes a ring or a part of the rattle may fall off due to friction.

The young and the venomous

The rattlesnake is ovoviviparous. The mother does not lay eggs in a nest. Instead, the eggs remain inside her body until they hatch. Baby rattlers can take care of themselves as soon as they're born. In some cases, they are more venomous than their parents.

■ Unlike other rattlesnakes, which prefer deserts or other arid regions, the timber rattlesnake is found in thick forests.

INTERESTING FACT!

Rattlesnakes thrust their way in water as they do on ground. They are excellent swimmers, and some of them may be spotted miles away from shore. Most rattlesnakes hold their rattles above water to keep them dry!

The Python

Not all snakes are poisonous. Pythons and boas are non-venomous. But they are big, strong and muscular. These snakes kill their prey by constricting, or squeezing it in their coils, until the prey suffocates.

Reticulated python

One of the longest of all snakes, it averages 16.4-26.2 feet (5-8 m), but can grow up to 33 feet (10 m)! It is found near the rivers and ponds of Southeast Asian jungles. The reticulated python is an excellent swimmer and tree climber. It is a nocturnal snake.

The rock python

The African and Indian rock pythons are famous for the beautiful patterns on their skin. They live among rocks and on trees. The Burmese rock python is a well-known sub-group of the Indian variety.

■ Some pythons exhibit a condition called albinism. An albino python might lack or not have enough melanin, the pigment that gives the snake its natural color. Albino pythons could be white, yellow, orange or brown. Most albinos have red eyes and tongues.

Green tree python

Compared to others in its family, the green tree python is slimmer and smaller. It mostly lives in trees and rarely climbs down. The bright green body of the snake helps it to hide among leaves and surprise its prey. It is hard to distinguish the green tree from the South American emerald tree boa. Both these snakes are very similar in color and habits.

■ Like all snakes, the python can stretch its jaws wide. But since the python has to hold onto its prey while killing it, their jaws are more rigid than those of the other snakes.

FACT FILE

Longest python
reticulated python: a specimen that was shot in Indonesia in 1912 measured 32 feet 9.5 inches (10 m)
Length of the rock python
18-20 feet (5.5-6 m)
Length of the royal python
3-6 feet (1-1.5 m)
Litter size of pythons
75 babies

INTERESTING FACT!

The giant African python that roamed the earth about 55 million years ago is considered to be the biggest snake that ever lived. It is believed that the snake was about 38.7 feet (11.8 m) long!

The royal and blood pythons

The royal python is found in Africa, and is one of the smaller pythons. It is also known as the ball python because of its ability to coil itself tightly into a ball when in danger. The blood python has irregular blood-red patterns on its skin. It is found in Southeast Asia. Its coloration helps it hide among branches and dead leaves.

■ Pythons are known to swallow animals as large as monkeys and caimans, animals similar to crocodiles.

Boas

Like pythons, boas also suffocate their prey before swallowing it whole. However, unlike pythons, boas hatch their eggs inside their body. They are the subject of many a horror jungle tale. Explorers have spun stories of having seen monster boas. In reality, they are shorter than pythons but much heavier.

■ Green anacondas are the world's heaviest snake. Growing up to 29.5 feet (9 m) in length, an adult green anaconda can be as heavy as 551 pounds (250 kg).

Common boa constrictor

This famous boa constrictor grows up to 11.5 feet (3.5 m) and is found in Central and South American jungles. Like all boas, it has powerful muscles and suffocates its prey. Bats are its favorite meal.

Anaconda

This is one of the most powerful predators in the animal kingdom and it can grow over 29.5 feet (9 m). It prefers still waters and marshy areas. Hence, it is also known as the water boa. Its eyes and nostrils are at the top of its head. This helps it move in the water without being seen. The anaconda's prey can be as large as pigs and deer.

Amazon tree boa

The Amazon tree boa is found in South American tropical forests. Its large pupils help this snake to hunt at night, while its slim body helps the boa to move swiftly on trees. It has a long striking range. It can hang from a branch and squeeze its prey in the air!

■ The anaconda's teeth are curved backward making it impossible for the prey to escape the powerful jaws once caught.

HABITAT

FACT FILE

Lifespan of boas
20-30 years
Number of young
20-60 born alive
Anaconda length
20-30 feet (6.1-9.1 m)
Boa constrictor average length
13 feet (4 m)

Other boas

The emerald tree boa is another tree-dwelling boa. Patterns on its skin help the snake to hide among the branches. The spotted sand boa hides in the sand and pounces on the unsuspecting prey.

■ When sunlight falls on the scales of a rainbow boa, the skin appears blue, green and violet, giving the snake its name.

Harmless Snakes

The word 'snake' rarely fails to frighten us. Yet most snakes are harmless. They usually bite to protect themselves, and even the ones that bite do not always inject venom.

■ Blind snakes live underground and look a lot like earthworms.

Kingsnake

Kingsnakes eat other snakes, including poisonous snakes such as rattlesnakes, coral snakes and copperheads. They are immune to the venom of these snakes. The milk snake is another variety of kingsnake. They eat almost anything, from small birds and rodents to lizards and other snakes. Most mimic snakes also belong to the kingsnake family. They are called mimic snakes because they copy the skin patterns of poisonous snakes, such as the coral snake, to ward off danger.

Rat snakes

These snakes are also called "chicken snakes" by farmers because they eat chicken eggs and chicks. However, their favorite food includes rats and mice, which they kill by squeezing. The black rat snake can grow to over 8.2 feet (2.5 m). Other kinds include the yellow, gray, and Texas rat snakes. Corn and fox snakes also belong to this family.

■ According to legend, milk snakes like to sneak into barns and suck milk from cows. That is how the snake got its name.

FACT FILE

The black rat snake can grow up to
8 feet (2.5 m) in length
Litter size of the kingsnake
4 to 20 babies
Length of the water snake
2-5 feet (0.66-1.64 m)
Litter size of garter snakes
50 babies
Lifespan of the hog-nosed snake
15-18 years

■ The red racer is a fast and non-venomous snake. Its diet consists of mice, small birds, lizards, insects and other snakes.

Hog-nosed snake

This harmless snake is very interesting. It hisses like a cobra when in danger, and pretends to strike. If that is not enough to put the enemy off, it writhes as if in pain and pretends to die! Frogs and toads are the favorite food of this snake.

Others in the family

Most snakes found in water are harmless. The bite of the common water snake is non-venomous, although blood could ooze out from the wound. Other harmless snakes include the garter snake, also known as garden or grass snake. Bull and racer snakes are valued by farmers because they help control the rat population.

■ When threatened, certain snakes, like this Monterey ring-necked snake, coil their tails tightly and elevate them to display their red undersides.

Enemies of the Snake

Predators make use of the fact that snakes are ground creatures and also cold-blooded. Snakes have to bask in the sun for energy, and cannot remain active for long. Their enemies know this and exhaust them before going in for the kill.

■ Snake charmers remove the snake's poisonous fangs after capturing it. This leads to mouth infections, eventually making the snake very ill. Since a dead snake is considered a bad omen, snake charmers release the snake before it dies. Without its fangs the snake does not survive for very long in the wild.

Killing without a cause

Humans are the snake's biggest enemies - they kill without cause. People usually kill snakes out of fear, not knowing that most snakes are harmless. Given the chance, snakes prefer to escape rather than strike. Humans have also destroyed a large number of snake habitats and eggs. Some snakes die as a result of being run over on our roads. Snakes are also killed for their skin. Snakeskin is used to make wallets, bags, shoes and other similar products. In some parts of the world, snakes are even eaten.

■ In China, the snake's gall bladder, meat, and skin are considered to have a lot of medicinal value. They are used to treat all kinds of diseases, from skin infections to mental illness. Many snakes are killed every year for this purpose.

■ The mongoose can defeat even the mighty king cobra. In fact, the mongoose is one of the king cobra's biggest enemies. It is known to eat the snake's eggs.

FACT FILE

Endangered snakes
Puerto Rican boa
Jamaican boa
Lake Erie water snake
King cobra
Indian rock python
Certain species of vipers
and rattlesnakes

INTERESTING FACT!

Mongooses are very good at fighting snakes and end up winning most of the time. They strike and bite with great speed, and have sharp reflexes. Moreover, snakes find it tough to bite through their thick coats.

Animal attack

Certain animals like badgers and weasels are major snake predators. Wild and domestic cats are also known to eat snakes. So are mongooses, large lizards and frogs. Raccoons, opossums and some ducks also feed on small snakes.

The pecking order

Most birds eat small snakes. Some birds peck the snake until it dies. These birds can easily spot a moving snake. The roadrunner is a well-known snake eater. Others include eagles, owls, hawks, kingfishers, peacocks, falcons, cranes and turkeys.

Glossary

Aggressive: Violent; hostile; unfriendly.

Anchor: Attach or fix.

Arid: Dry; having little or no rainfall.

Camouflage: The ability of some animals to remain hidden, usually because of their likeness to the surroundings.

Cold-blooded: Unable to self-maintain body temperature

Combat: Struggle; fight.

Constrict: To squeeze.

Distinguish: To tell apart; differentiate.

Elevate: Raise or lift up.

Enzyme: A complex protein that speeds up chemical reactions.

Equipped: Provided with what is necessary.

Evolution: The process by which the traits of a species change over a long period of time, as animals with the traits best suited to their environment survive and reproduce.

Exhaust: To tire out.

Expandable: Stretchable; flexible.

Fatal: Lethal; deadly; causing death.

Feces: Solid waste of animals.

Foliage: Plants.

Frequent: Regular in occurrence.

Gall bladder: A muscular sac that is a part of the liver and stores bile.

Habitat: Natural home of an animal or plant.

Hazard: Danger; risk.

Immune: Not affected by something.

Juvenile: Young.

Keeled: Having a ridge or shaped like a ridge.

Marine: Of or relating to the sea.

Melanin: A black or dark brown pigment found in the hair, eyes and skin of animals and humans.

Mimic: To copy.

Musk: A strong-smelling secretion of the male musk deer; anything that has a similar smell.

New World: The western hemisphere: the Americas.

Nocturnal: Of or relating to night; animals or birds that come out into the open at night.

Old World: The eastern hemisphere: Europe, Asia and Africa.

Oriental: Of or relating to countries in the East and Far East, such as India, China and the Philippines.

Predator: A carnivorous animal

Refined: Advanced.

Reflex: Reaction; spontaneous response.

Resemble: To look alike; to be similar.

Semi-arid: Area with low rainfall and little vegetation.

Sophisticated: Developed; advanced.

Suffocate: To choke; to kill by not allowing to breathe.

Tactic: Strategy; plan.

Three-dimensional (3D): Having or relating to the three dimensions – length, height and width.

Warm-blooded: Having a body temperature that does not change with that of the surroundings.

Further Reading

Books

Hoff, Mary. *Snakes.* Mankato, MN.: Creative Education, 2007.

Huggins-Cooper, Lynn. *Slithering Snakes.* Smart Apple Media, 2007.

Mason, Adrienne. *Snakes.* Toronto: Kids Can Press, 2005.

Internet Addresses

The Antiguan Racer Conservation Project
http://www.antiguanracer.org/html/home.htm

King Cobra
http://www.nationalgeographic.com/features/97/kingcobra/index-n.html

National Geographic: Reptiles
http://animals.nationalgeographic.com/animals/reptiles.html

San Diego Zoo: Snake
http://www.sandiegozoo.org/animalbytes/t-snake.html

Index